# INSTANT KUNDALINI

*Open your Third eye with this amazing step-by-step guide. Transform your life by controlling your Chakras, mastering your Kundalini and enhancing your Intuition.*

By

GREGORY J ROBERTS

## Chakras and Kundalini

Like a rainbow in the sky, your chakras are a rainbow of energy within you. The colour of each chakra represents a different layer or dimension of you. I speak about six chakras in this book. Your root chakra, which is red in colour and found at the base of your spine, your sacral chakra, which is orange and located in your stomach area, your solar plexus chakra, which is yellow and located in your solar plexus area, your heart chakra, which is green and located near your heart, your throat chakra, which is blue and located in your throat area, and your third eye, which is indigo and located just above your eyes.

Kundalini energy brings your chakras to life. This very powerful energy lies dormant at the base of your spine. When awakened, the energy flows upwards from your root chakra to your third eye, activating and balancing each chakra as this energy passes through.

These chakras exist in everyone, although you could live a lifetime without even knowing that they exist.

These six chakras are the main operating system of your inner space, and once you awaken them, you will have much more control over many different aspects of your life.

You could work on each chakra individually and try to identify your personal blocks and never awaken your kundalini. The main focus of this book is to guide you through a step-by-step process that awakens, activates, and connects all of your chakras in order, permanently, with no blocks. Your kundalini awakens in your root chakra and flows up, step-by-step, chakra by chakra, building on one another and connecting your kundalini to your third eye. The process of activating and connecting all of your chakras, in order, is called a kundalini awakening. As the energy moves from your root chakra up to your third eye, your kundalini finds its final destination here.

# Table of Contents

Introduction .................................................................. 1

**Chapter 1**
Root Chakra (Finding Now) ................................................. 7

**Chapter 2**
Sacral Chakra (Finding You) ............................................. 12

**Chapter 3**
Solar Plexus (Finding Others) ........................................... 17

**Chapter 4**
The Mind (Your Main Block) ............................................. 22

**Chapter 5**
Heart Chakra (Your Real Mind) .......................................... 27

**Chapter 6**
Throat Chakra (The Ultimate Chakra) ................................. 32

**Chapter 7**
Third Eye (Seeing Clearly) .............................................. 38

## Introduction

I have created a step-by-step process that has the power to instantly awaken your kundalini. I will guide you through seven realizations that will help connect you to each of your chakras and understand the purpose each one has in your life. Through understanding these spiritual truths, you can supercharge your energy, awaken each chakra, and allow your kundalini energy to rise higher and higher, from your root chakra up to your third eye.

There is nothing magical in the process of awakening your kundalini. There is no yoga pose or any certain frequency you can listen to, no one meditation or drug you can use to awaken your kundalini. You don't need to spend thousands of dollars on teachers or spend a lifetime studying or searching for answers in foreign lands. I will share my step-by-step process, in an easy-to-read and understand way, to self-actualize and awaken your kundalini. This book gives you the tools and the know-how to instantly awaken your kundalini and lead a much more fulfilling life.

After a decade, my main focus is on learning how to heal the body's energy, chakras, and teaching kundalini to my clients. Most people are familiar with the hands-on healing of reiki. I studied Reiki Healing, became a Reiki Master, and added this modality to my healing practice. I was practicing reiki for some time and was finding that this form of energy healing was helpful to my clients, although the effects were temporary. In general, people seeking reiki healing would come back, over and over again. I was seeing it as a temporary fix. After the treatment, they would feel great for a certain period of time. Although, after the effects of the treatment wore off and some time passed, life would undoubtedly hit them again, their energy would be thrown off, and they would begin the process, day by day, of getting closer to needing another treatment. I didn't see much long-term benefit or enlightenment in this healing process. Reiki, alone, created a cycle that could allow people to experience the same issues and blocks that needed healing, over and over again. I wanted to play a role in helping my clients fully heal. The reiki healing was a good addition to my practice, although it wasn't totally fulfilling the purpose and vision of my work.

Before embarking on reiki and energy healing, I spent many years using Hypnotherapy, Past Life Regression, and Neuro-Linguistic Programming. I had been working with clients in therapy, helping them to heal different aspects of their lives. I taught about spiritual awakening and helped clients use the law of attraction. I experienced quite amazing results with my clients while using these modalities in my healing practice. Years of using these therapies had given me invaluable experience. I realized that this combination of modalities is also energy work. As I was helping my clients shift their thoughts and beliefs, they were also creating huge energy shifts within themselves, healing their minds, bodies, and awakening their chakras. Their spiritual healing had the power to heal them both mentally and physically. The subtle changes they made in their beliefs shifted their energy in so many ways. I was very familiar with the connections between the subconscious mind and the conscious mind, the vibration of words, thoughts, energy, chakras, kundalini, the energetic operation of the body and its effects on health, and the potential each person has to transform every aspect of their life.

All of the many modalities that I was using were all starting to come together and I knew that it was creating something special. By incorporating everything I had learned, through providing therapy, with the power of hands-on healing, I could accelerate the process of healing for my clients. It had become clear to me that my new path of healing would be to incorporate all of this knowledge into a therapeutic and hands-on approach to healing. This new modality would focus energy work on the chakras, combined with an in-depth teaching of kundalini. I spent many years meditating on my own chakras and had only learned the basics from books. Most of what I learned was directly obtained from meditating on my own chakras and self-reflecting. Through years of devotion, I received a very clear diagram of my inner workings, the function of my chakras, and many spiritual truths obtained, directly from my heart. I have combined many healing modalities, years of experience with clients, and everything I have personally learned in my life, to create a unique modality of kundalini energy work and spiritual teachings, to assist people in healing and awakening their chakras and kundalini.

I created this as a very enhanced and focused version of reiki, in which I focus the energy work on each chakra while teaching kundalini. I wanted to create masters. I wanted my treatments to be permanent. Through each client's own personal awakening, this would allow them to be in control of all aspects of their life. I wanted them to become master energy healers of themselves, and in the process, lose the need for me as their guide as they empower themselves. Masters creating masters was my philosophy. With years of experience, my own kundalini awakening, and thousands of success stories, it is my honour and privilege to share my unique, step-by-step process of awakening the kundalini with you, through this book, so you too, like thousands of others, can have your own permanent and instant kundalini experience and become the master of your life.

Through the repetition of hands-on healing and energy work every day for over ten years, the Instant Kundalini process has been born and refined into easy-to-understand ideas that you can implement into your daily life. It doesn't matter where you are, your circumstances, or your life challenges, you can instantly unlock your chakras and the full power of your kundalini. After a decade in the making and perfecting this step-by-step guide with thousands of clients, I am humbled and honoured to share with you The Instant Kundalini Process. From my heart to yours, I deliver a unique process, the wisdom obtained directly from the hands of a healer, and written for you by the same hands.

# CHAPTER I

## Root Chakra (Finding Now)

Your root chakra has three dimensions—your past, your future, and the present moment. You experience your life somewhere in between. If you think about it, most of the time you are thinking about something that has happened in your past, or you are daydreaming about something that could possibly happen in your future. The accumulation of your past experiences gives your mind the information it needs to imagine up these future experiences. The future experiences that you fantasize about and the ones that you fear are all projections being created by your past. You are going to find your way out of your past and out of your future in a quest to find the present moment.

Ask yourself these questions: Who would you be with no past? Who would you be if your mind was erased and wiped clean? Take a moment to think about this. The answer is, you would be no one, although, at the same time, you could be anyone. This is powerful. The last time you would have felt this was the second that you were born. The second that you were born, you had no past experience, nothing to be judged by or to predict your future. We will always tell a baby that he can do anything with his life. The baby has no past experience to predict his future. Feeling this is the key, release your past and release your future and find what's left. Find the moment happening right now, in this exact second. Loosen the tight grip that you are holding on your past, and loosen the tight grip that you are holding on your future.

Even just for a moment, if you can release your past and release your future, you can find the space that resides directly in between—the NOW.

In the NOW, nothing is happening and nothing can reach you, where you are free from your past and future. In the present moment, you will find the natural state of bliss. It's a feeling of unconditional love. It is a natural state that has always existed in you. Deep inside where nothing is happening, and for no reason at all, other than that it is your natural state. This is where you started. The state you were in before you created the illusion, and the story of who and what you are. The State of Pure Bliss.

For most people, their past has created an abundance of jagged edges. It's hard to get rooted on the jagged edges of your past. You need a solid foundation to grow and fully activate your root chakra. Use this visualization to help you work on it.

Visualize a cement mixer pouring concrete on all of your past experiences. See the cement covering all of the jagged edges of your past, until your past is completely buried. Notice the cement getting hard, flat, and smooth. See this solid foundation and stand on it. All of your past experiences are still there, although they are all buried deep in the concrete. The only thing that can reach you NOW is the wisdom from the experiences and the know-how of your past. As you release the old, you can become anything you wish to be. Stand tall on your new foundation as you activate your root chakra. Become rooted and grounded in the here and now. Feel the foundation beneath you and feel the potential above you! With every step you take, become more rooted and grounded, and with every step you take, become more and more alive.

Release the past and release your future. Find your natural state of happiness and love. Find NOW. No one is responsible for your happiness and no one is responsible to give you love. It is an inside job. It is your responsibility. To do this, connect to your natural state of being, find bliss, then go on with your life. Your happiness is not created by the actions of others, the day that you are having, or the obstacles that are on your path. Love and happiness is just who you are. Come back to NOW as often as you can. The closer you are to NOW, the closer you are to love and happiness. With your root chakra activated, this is your natural state, existing in you, for no reason, where nothing is happening. It's just who you are.

Finding NOW is what activates your root chakra and opens the door for your kundalini energy to flow up to your sacral chakra. As you move on in the book, move on with a feeling of being born again and temporarily leave your past and future experiences behind.

# CHAPTER 2

## Sacral Chakra (Finding You)

Your sacral chakra is all about your relationship with yourself. It has two dimensions. How you view yourself and how you treat yourself.

When you were born, you could be anyone. Your past has locked you into thinking that only one version of you exists, although, in reality, millions of different versions of you exist and you have settled for this one. If you were to change any aspect of your past experience, it would completely change who you are. You have the same unlimited potential that you had when you were born, although it has been hidden under the thin layer of your past experience and the narrow view of your future.

Can you think of yourself as someone else? Can you think of a different version of you? Can you think of the best version of you? Replace the old version of you with the best version of you and it's like you have plugged in a new microchip and changed your whole operating system. Every cell in your body, every molecule in the universe responds to the version of you that you plug in and claim. When you peel off the layers of your past and your thoughts about your future, you find the present moment. In the NOW, without the perception of your past and future, you can see your true self and your true potential. You want to make changes to your perceived self. Your self-image is the main microchip of your operating system. Activate your sacral chakra by plugging in the best version of you. When you do this, you not only change yourself, you also change the entire universe.

Take some time now to visualize the best version of you. What would the happiest version of you look like? What would the healthiest version of you look like? Or the richest version of you? The version of you with the best relationships? Or the version of you with the best career, the most patient you, kind, sharing, caring, compassionate you, the unlimited you who is willing to grow in every area of your life, in every direction, with no boundaries or borders, needing no one to believe in or to love you, except you. The possibilities are endless with this visualization. Create the best image of yourself that you can possibly imagine. Redefine how you see yourself by redefining your self-image and plugging in the best you.

You must take full responsibility for your life. Make no excuses and hold no one else responsible. I mean FULL responsibility… you are responsible for your life! You are responsible for your happiness! Your happiness is not reliant on other people or how they treat you, what your day holds for you, or what situations you encounter throughout the day. Take responsibility for your happiness, never put it in the hands of anyone else. You are in charge of a good day or a bad day, a good life or a bad life. Your happiness is no one's responsibility but your own. Happiness is your natural state, inside, where nothing is happening and for no reason at all. Let this set the stage for your day. You are responsible for your happiness, it's a choice, not a possible outcome. People and situations do not control your happiness, you do. When you lose your course, simply come back to NOW and find the natural state of bliss that you are.

You don't need anyone to complete you, you have to complete yourself. The people in your life are not there to complete you, they are there to complement you, and you are not there to complement them. When you are whole and complete, on your own, no one can break you. If you allow other people to complete you, in their absence, you will become incomplete. Know that you are whole and complete on your own, and that the ultimate relationship in your life is the one you have with yourself. The better you treat yourself, the better you are able to treat others. Do not empty your cup onto others, fill your cup first, then let it spill over onto everyone around you and your cup will always be full.

Think about someone you love. Do you let others speak badly to them or hurt them? Do you want the best for them? You must love yourself even more than you love them. Your life begins and ends with you. It's not what you do for others, it's what you do for yourself that truly matters. Your relationship with yourself is the ultimate relationship in your life.

Activate your sacral chakra by finding the best you and the kundalini can rise to your solar plexus chakra.

# CHAPTER 3

## Solar Plexus (Finding Others)

Visualize one hundred people standing around a large campfire. If everyone were to take a picture, each person would believe that they have the photo of the fire. Their photo is only one small angle, just one fractional view of the fire. I want you to realize that the true picture of the fire is not viewed from one angle, it's viewed from all angles, it is the collection of every person's photo that creates the complete view of the fire.

You can use this visualization for all the different situations in your life that involve the views of others. If you believe your view is the ultimate view, the views of others become less valid or even wrong to you, since their views are not in alignment with your own. We are all viewing life from our own valid and unique angles and perspectives. We have to accept the fact that everyone has a different view and allow this natural process to take place. You cannot fight it, you cannot prove that everyone is wrong so that you feel right, or the conflicts would never end in your life. To awaken your solar plexus chakra, practice stepping out of your individual view with total acceptance, allowing yourself to see all situations from every direction and angle. Look at life through as many eyes as you can, other than your own. You will find no conflict, only growth, expansion, and deep learning.

When you think that you know something, you actually become stuck, you get locked into your own unique view, thinking it is the ultimate. You want the opposite. You want to grow. When you can stop talking and start listening, you will grow. Look at your relationship with everyone from this perspective, and you will never stop learning as everyone will always have their own unique view of things—sometimes quite different from yours. This gives you a constant opportunity to practice acceptance and an unlimited opportunity to learn, grow, and become wise.

No one can understand you, and you cannot understand anyone. Strive to get this absolutely clear. No one can understand you and you can never, no matter how hard you try, understand anyone else. We are all too unique to understand. Our experiences, what we have learned, encountered, and lived through are all very different and unique. It is okay to think the way that we think based on our own personal experience, although we cannot judge anyone else's experience. It is impossible, unless we have lived their life in its entirety. We are right to believe what we believe, although if we believe our own view is the ultimate view, we will judge the view of others.

Awaken your solar plexus with acceptance, unconditional love, and by believing in the ability of others to become the best version of themselves. Accept that a unique view exists in everyone. If you are willing to let go of what you think is right, you will grow. Through listening, taking a sincere interest in people, and seeing life from as many different perspectives as possible, your own perspective will grow. The more angles that you view life through, the bigger your view becomes. Shed the disease of judgment and make the shift to acceptance and unconditional love.

From your personal situation to the collective experience of humanity, almost eight billion different views exist around the world. Each person, with a different life experience, living in a different country, surrounded by a different belief system, will have a different view. Whether it be politics, religion, relationships, the different ways to live, different family values... the list is endless. Let go of your unique, very narrow view, step back and see how beautiful and unique the whole world really is. From this grand view, you can see a world in which no one needs to be judged, classified, labelled, or made to feel wrong. From this view, you can see that each person simply needs and deserves to be loved, accepted, and believed in. One thing you will notice that everyone has in common is that they want to be accepted, believed in, and loved. When you awaken the solar plexus, you can respect and accept that everyone on Earth has a unique view.

Many believe the solar plexus chakra is yellow. My personal belief is that it is gold. I like to visualize myself sending golden light out to everyone and everything, feeling unconditional love and feeling acceptance, flowing from myself and being received by everyone and everything. I wish everyone the best in life and hope that everyone finds their own happiness. I hope that everyone will find the best version of themselves, the one that you are finding in yourself today.

As the Kundalini Energy flows up from your solar plexus chakra, most would think your heart chakra is the next destination, although your mind is blocking its path.

# CHAPTER 4

## The Mind (Your Main Block)

We spend years in counselling or coaching, trying to heal our pasts. We meditate to find the present moment. We use positive thinking and attempt to use the law of attraction to visualize ourselves and our futures the way that we would like them. We use affirmations, working on self-love, on loving others, and still, with all this work, we feel as though we may have missed the breakthrough and we are still a long way away from finding true happiness or life's purpose. Even after putting in this much effort, many people get stuck here and do not make it past this point, spending the rest of their lives in this cycle of self-improvement and finding little result. This is helpful, although, inside, we know that there is still more.

*Instant Kundalini*

Your mind has been managing all aspects of your life, such as your past, your future, your relationships with yourself, and your relationships with others. Your mind keeps your thoughts spinning, and without knowing it, your lower chakras have been empowered by your mind.

What most will never find is that the mind cloaks itself over your heart, rendering the light of your heart useless as the mind completely runs the show, so much so that you think you are your mind.

Strive to understand this. This is deep, but you must get it. Your mind is not you. Your mind is just a function of your brain; your mind is using your imagination and past experiences to compare people, places, and things in so many different ways. The mind's function is to enhance your decision-making ability. Your mind is proficient at comparing everything and everyone to yourself and your unique view on life. This constant comparing and judging of the mind has been your main block. Your mind cannot make decisions, it plays and replays, over and over, until you decide or tell it to stop.

You have given your past, your future, all your relationships, even the one with yourself, to your mind. Without knowing it, your mind has been on autopilot, playing out imagined scenarios in all areas of your life. Over and over again, your mind is comparing, judging, and imagining at a very steady pace. Life is scary, stressful, and confusing, with your mind at the helm. Literally, your mind has been your ultimate invalid psychic, predicting every aspect of your life. You have been so stuck in your mind that it feels impossible to get out.

This is the point at which many people become stuck. You can stay at this point for a lifetime, although, if you follow these steps, you are about to be free! Your mind is not you, it has made you live in your imagination. All of the answers that you have been looking for have been hiding in plain sight, right in front of you. The secret is your heart. It has been tucked away so tightly that it has become inaccessible. Your mind has taken full control

## Instant Kundalini

of all areas of your life. Understand that your heart is your true master and guide. Your heart has been patiently waiting to take over your life completely and shine down on all areas of your life that have never seen the light before. You are about to be free!

With this visualization, you are going to do a delicate psychic surgery on yourself. Your mind has been covering your heart. You are going to remove the thin layer of your mind that has been secretly covering every inch of your heart. I want you to feel your mind, thinly wrapped around your heart, like a black or grey film of energy that has taken control of your heart and blocked all of your heart's abilities. Your mind is the cloud that has been blocking the sunlight of your heart from shining down on all areas of your life. You have the power to command your mind to leave your heart space. Demand your mind to leave your heart, and for now, simply send it away. Tell your mind that you do not need it and to stay away and be quiet for now. See your mind floating away. Now, notice that your heart has become free and that it is fully awakened, unrestricted, and is now allowing the kundalini energy to flow into your heart space for the very first time in your life. This psychic surgery that you performed on yourself has allowed your kundalini energy to rush in and rise to the sacred heart space—unrestricted and free-flowing. The mind has kept you in a maze and now your heart will set you free.

## CHAPTER 5

### Heart Chakra (Your Real Mind)

When the heart chakra is activated, the true kundalini awakening begins. Your lower chakras are activated in a way that was never possible before. They have a new master that gives them the reflection of love. With your mind at rest, through the lens of your heart, your chakras come to life. Your heart has held the key.

If you look at your past through your mind, you will play your past over and over again. When you look at your past through your heart, you lose the need to judge your past or your experiences. You can accept everything that has happened to you as it has all brought you to this point in your life. You have created wisdom in the process, and your past holds your wisdom.

When you look at your future through your mind, it can be unclear and frightening. When you view your future through your heart, you realize that you are the creator, you are safe, and that your future holds unlimited potential.

When you look at yourself through your mind, you see your flaws. When you look at yourself through your heart, you can love yourself. When you look in the mirror through your mind's eye, you are looking at yourself through the eyes of everyone else. When you look at yourself through your heart, you can finally see yourself. From this view, you can fall in love with the unique and beautiful you that is full of potential and growing in every area of your life.

When you look at others through your mind, you could spend a lifetime analyzing and judging them, their choices, and their actions. When you look at others through your heart, you can see that everyone simply wants to be accepted, believed in, and loved.

With your mind at rest, your heart shines down on all of your chakras and on all areas of your life. When you look through your heart, you get a clear view of unconditional love. For most, the heart is locked and the mind is controlling every aspect of their lives. When you are faced with a challenge, your mind will play it over and over again. When you bring a challenge into your awakened heart space, the clear view of unconditional love will give you crystal clear answers. Any problem can be solved with love. The reflection of love from your heart chakra fully activates your lower chakras. They cannot be activated by your mind. The heart is what enables the kundalini energy to flow, unrestricted, through the lower chakras. The heart unlocks the spiritual truths in you, providing this reflection from your heart to your root, sacral, and solar plexus chakras. When your lower chakras are connected to your heart chakra, this creates your inner space. You do your inner work in your inner space with love.

As the kundalini moves through your heart, it awakens your throat chakra. Your mind has been in charge of your throat, your voice, your thoughts, and your beliefs. With your mind in control, you cannot activate your throat chakra. Your throat chakra will only awaken when the energy passes through the heart and into the throat.

When you bypass your heart, you speak from your mind. You have been thinking and speaking from your mind, not from your heart. This will be your greatest shift. Look through your heart, connect with love, compassion, understanding, acceptance, caring, sharing, and gratitude. This will allow you to see life for what it is, with no judgment and with complete acceptance. For the few, with the heart unlocked, this will allow the kundalini energy to rise to a place that most will never feel. Your kundalini rises from your lower chakras, directly into your open, unfiltered heart, and then into your throat chakra. Then, you can willingly speak the beautiful truths of your heart. The heart chakra has the power to transform and purify every aspect of your life. Once your kundalini energy rises to your throat chakra and these two chakras become connected, you start to think and speak directly from your heart.

## CHAPTER 6

### Throat Chakra (The Ultimate Chakra)

Your heart chakra gives birth to your throat chakra. As you use your heart to view all aspects of your life, as you problem-solve with unconditional love and learn to speak directly from your heart space, your kundalini rises.

Your throat chakra is more than just the voice with which you speak. It is also the voice that has created your thoughts and your beliefs. It is possible to spend a lifetime thinking and speaking from your mind and totally miss the activation of your heart and throat chakras.

Your throat chakra could be considered a magical chakra. It impacts every cell in your body. You need to master the power of words. Every word you speak, think, or believe carries a unique vibration. Visualize one positive word or one negative word being spoken, and in response to that word, notice how that one word can vibrate every single cell of your entire body. Please take a few minutes to really feel this. Beautiful words vibrate with health, and negative words vibrate with disease. How do you want to vibrate? The voice within your throat chakra is creating the vibration of you, and on a deeper level, it is creating the program that runs every system in your body. Own your words, let them flow freely through your heart, let them be beautiful. The negative words that you speak return to you and become you. Master your throat, and you master all aspects of your life. From your heart, you speak the truth and you do it in the most loving way. From your heart, you speak beautifully about yourself and everyone else. From your heart, you can speak beautifully about everything. Your beautiful words will pay you back immensely as your throat overflows, vibrating with health and love, through every cell in your body.

What are you willing to speak into existence? What are you willing to claim? What are you willing to believe in? I will teach you how to use your voice to command everything you want into reality. Let us start with your body. I will let you in on one of life's secrets. Each person's body operates in a different way. You have a unique program. It is like your unique operating system. It has been created by you, and that program can be changed by you with the help of your voice, throat chakra, and the magical power of water.

I will teach you about the magical power of water. One thing that you will find in every cell of your body is water. Did you know that water has memory? Did you know that if you send a thought to a cup of water, the water itself will change its structure? The water takes the vibration of your words, thoughts, and beliefs and turns it into a program that provides data within your cells. That data is programming the organs in your body, giving them their unique operation and function. The water in each and every cell of your body is the programmable link between your voice and your unique operating system. When you understand this, you can see that what you believe in, you will surely become. What are the words you use to describe your body? What are your beliefs on diet, nutrition, and your body's ability to digest food? What are your beliefs on losing weight, building muscle, or your body's ability to heal? Your words, your thoughts, and your beliefs are your program.

As an example, if you eat a cookie and you believe that you will gain weight in a certain area, you have created a belief. That belief creates the program that structures the water in your body, giving signals to your cells and organs. This makes your beliefs a functioning reality and you do gain weight where you believed you would. What if you believed that your body could easily, fully digest any food?

With this realization, take full ownership and responsibility for rewriting your program and to make a shift in your words, thoughts, and beliefs.

Exercise: Fill up a glass cup of water. Set it in front of you. Say the word "love" ten times and focus on the cup of water. Now, without speaking out loud, think of the word "love" ten times and focus the energy on the cup of water. You have just programmed water for the first time. This simple process of sending the vibration of love, healing, or anything you wish to your water before you drink it, will dramatically transform its program, structure, and effect on your body. The program and the structure of the water that you drink is just as important as your need to drink water, although, for the most part, you have paid little or no attention to it. Learning to program water outside of you gives you the exact skill you need to transform the water inside of you and the water inside of others. This meditation, with some practice, is an advanced form of energy healing that you can perform on yourself and others.

Your throat chakra is the ultimate power source and you are the master. Use the power of your throat chakra to send love and healing through your words, thoughts, and new beliefs. Use your throat chakra to become a healer of water and start healing the water in your cells, your organs, the energy in and around you and everyone in your life. Once you activate your heart and throat chakras, you have the ability to transform the energy of every cell inside yourself and everyone around you. Even the energy in the spaces in which you spend time will increasingly become more beautiful, peaceful, and full of love.

Bring all aspects of your life into your heart space, use your heart to reflect on your past, your future, your relationship with yourself and others, and all problems can easily be solved, painlessly and with love. Speak and also listen with care, compassion, understanding, acceptance, and unconditional love. Allow this powerful kundalini energy to flow from your lower chakras up through your heart, awakening the kundalini in your throat chakra as it passes through. As all your chakras are lining up for the very first time, your kundalini has a clear path to flow, sending your kundalini energy through your throat chakra and up to your third eye.

## CHAPTER 7

### Third Eye (Seeing Clearly)

Your third eye is born by the awakening of the chakras that we have covered. Each one of your chakras plays a unique role in opening your third eye. You need each one awakened, in this order, to see life with a clear view. As you release the grasp on your past and future and find Now, use the reflection of your heart to love, accept, and believe in yourself, and with that same reflection, find the ability to love, accept, and believe in others. Letting go of judgment, as your natural reflex, will become acceptance. Let your truths flow through your heart and to your throat. Speak these truths directly from your heart, in the frequency of love, to heal your body, to heal your relationships, and to heal your life.

Your physical eyes see life from one angle. Your third eye allows you to see life clearly and completely from all angles. When you look through your third eye, you will see a whole new world. By using this step-by-step process, it will allow your third eye to remain permanently open and active in your life. With your third eye open, your life instantly becomes more peaceful, beautiful, easier, and slower moving. An open third eye will fill your life with love, gratitude, acceptance, hope, passion, and desire. You will tap into new levels of creativity and explore new levels and aspects of yourself that have been unexplored or long forgotten. Start your life over again. You have been given a new life within a life. Your third eye is not metaphysical, it is complete clarity.

When the kundalini rises to your third eye, it has reached its destination. The opening of your third eye signifies the highest level of your inner work, pertaining to this life, in this dimension. All truths and the answers to life's situations and challenges become clear and the need to feed your mind anything, other than love, subsides. All of the answers that you have been looking for are not found in books, courses, or other people's stories. All of the answers to all of life's questions are inside of you. They have been there the whole time, in simple form, waiting for you to discover and uncover. You can see what most will fail to see, in every situation, this will be part of your normal view.

You are awakened. Your kundalini has risen to its destination. This book may be short, but these are the basics to awaken your kundalini. This is all the knowledge that you need to continue the work on your own. You are a master and the world is now your teacher. Let yourself grow with everything you encounter, from this point forward, for the rest of your life. Use this step-by-step process, every day, to refresh and awaken your chakras with the simplicity that I have conveyed. Life will give you endless opportunities to use this knowledge, to cultivate all of your chakras, in all ways and in all directions.

*Instant Kundalini*

Awakening Date

Date:

Signature:

CPSIA information can be obtained
at www.ICGtesting.com
Printed in the USA
LVHW080857051021
699562LV00002B/148